To the DeBoer Family

With this book I want you to
know that you have unknown
friends all over the world
who love the positive spirit
of your people & your country

with love,
Mary

UNITED STATES OF AMERICA

CHIEF OF STATE AND GOVERNMENT: PRESIDENT
POPULATION (2001): 278,058,881
LAND USE (2001): ARABLE LAND 19%
PERMANENT PASTURES 25%
FORESTS AND WOODLAND 30%
OTHER 26%
FAMILY: PART OF THE GLOBAL FAMILY OF
NEW ZEALAND AND THE WORLD.

NEW ZEALAND

CHIEF OF STATE: BRITISH MONARCH,
REPRESENTED BY THE GOVERNOR-GENERAL
HEAD OF GOVERNMENT: PRIME MINISTER
POPULATION (2001): 3,737,277
LAND USE (2000): PASTURE AND ARABLE LAND 43.8%
PLANTED PRODUCTION FOREST 6.6%
NATURAL FOREST 23.1%
OTHER 26.5%
FAMILY: PART OF THE GLOBAL FAMILY OF
AMERICA AND THE WORLD.

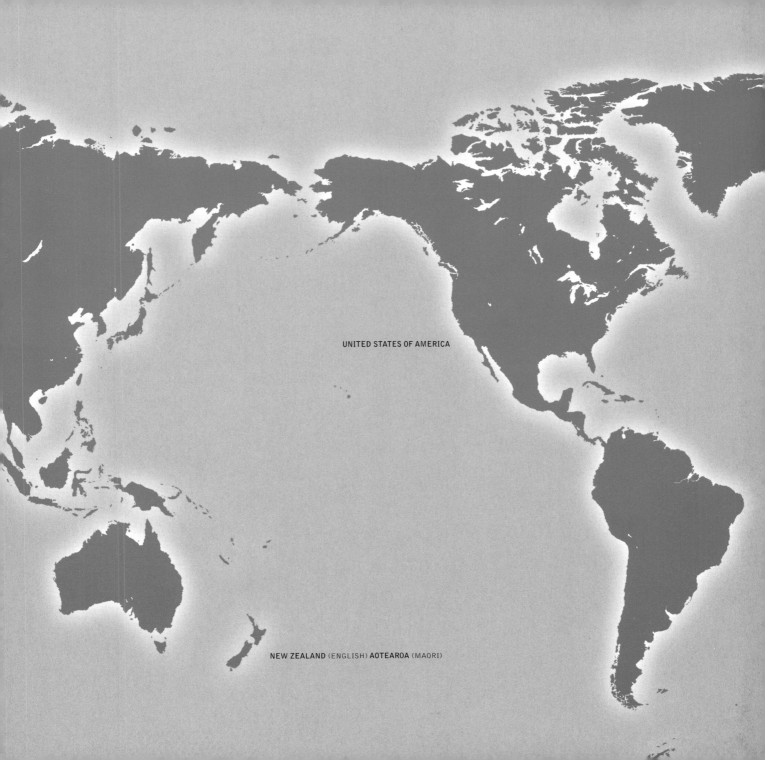

UNITED STATES OF AMERICA

NEW ZEALAND (ENGLISH) AOTEAROA (MAORI)

INSPIRED AND EDITED BY MARY HOBBS

PUBLISHED BY NEW ZEALAND OUTSIDE LTD

PO Box 17673 Sumner, Christchurch, New Zealand

Email: nzoutside@xtra.co.nz

First published January 2002

ISBN   0-473-08301-9

Printed in New Zealand
Rangiora Print, Christchurch

Previous books/publications:

Kiwi Tucker for the Soul™
www.kiwitucker.com

New Zealand Outside
Annual since 1995. Bi-annual since 2002
www.nzoutside.com

After costs, a percentage of the funds of this book will be
donated to the children of America and Afghanistan who
have lost parents in the recent tragedies.

Letters to New York and America

From New Zealand with Love

MARY HOBBS

To those incredible people who inspire the world through their actions of bravery and courage, and who have not hesitated to risk their own lives in efforts to save others.

To those who do what they can to create a positive difference in the world, and to those who — regardless of race, religion or culture — work at creating a world of harmony and peace for all.

FOREWORD

 When I think of America...

When I think of America I think of the founding documents of your country.

I think of the Bill of Rights and the Declaration of Independence.

I think of a nation where dreams can come true if one is prepared to work hard enough and if one refuses to give up.

When I think of America I think of movies with inspiring people and happy endings, of love stories and adventures where the heroes always overcome great odds and make their dreams a reality.

When I think of America I think of the impossible becoming possible.

When I think of America I think of your patriotism and pride and the spirit of a people who – in the face of great tragedy – joined together and showed the world real heroes, and demonstrated a strength of real spirit that lit every single corner of the world.

When I think of my American friends I think of warm, wonderful people who welcome our family with open hearts and who willingly share their homes, their world and their lives with us.

When I think of Americans I think of family.

So when your tragedies occurred on September 11 – it was also our tragedy.

I wanted to help.

I was here and you were there.

We flew the American flag from our office. We sent positive thoughts of well-being to you.

It helped but we didn't feel it was enough.

Then the idea for this book arrived – unannounced – at dinner one night and simply refused to go away. I told my husband Charlie and we've been working on it together ever since.

The book contains letters of hope and inspiration from some outstanding New Zealanders who willingly set aside the time to be photographed and to contribute beautiful messages to the American people half a world away. They truly touch the heart.

I hope this book finds its way into the lives of our unknown friends in America who are suffering and gives you comfort. I hope it touches your heart and sprinkles you with a little magic. And I hope it brings the world a little closer, linking countries together through all that is truly great about the spirit of people reaching out to each other.

This is our gift to you – our American family.

From New Zealand – with love.

Mary

Mary Hobbs

'You do not know us . . .

we are half a world away

but we are family'

GOVERNMENT HOUSE
New Zealand

Message to the People of America

The events of September 11 2001 in the United States of America were a stark reminder of the fragility of peace and the value of every human life, regardless of race, creed or culture.

The thousands of people who lost their lives on that date, as a result of acts of terrorism, were mothers, fathers, brothers, sisters, sons and daughters. The world feels enormous sadness for the families of those left behind, as it does for all victims of war and terrorism around the globe.

On behalf of all New Zealanders, I wish the people of the United States of America strength in recovering from the events of September 11, and the courage to remain a nation committed to justice and peace.

Silvia Cartwright

The Honourable Dame Silvia Cartwright PCNZM, DBE
Governor-General of New Zealand

 Prime Minister

To the American people

New Zealanders were deeply shaken by the appalling terrorist attacks on New York, Washington DC and Pennsylvania on 11 September 2001. They were acts of utterly incomprehensible violence that shook us all profoundly.

In the aftermath, all New Zealanders joined with me in expressing our regrets to the victims of these horrendous acts – the people in the towers, the Pentagon and on the planes, passers-by caught in the attacks, those caught up while in the line of duty such as the fire-fighters, the police officers, and the ambulance personnel, and all their families and friends.

There can be no tolerance of such horrific acts of terrorism. It is important that the international community now works together to combat terrorism. New Zealand has offered diplomatic, intelligence, and military support and will ensure that its financial systems are closed to terrorists. We have also stepped up our humanitarian aid to the Afghan people.

The United States and the rest of the world will never forget the tragedy of 11 September. We know, however, that the vitality, determination, and strength of spirit of the American people will enable them to overcome the challenges posed by those awful events. We must all work together to prevent such horrific acts in the future and to create a more peaceful world.

Yours sincerely

Helen Clark
Prime Minister

'In...conflicts of the twentieth century,
New Zealanders and Americans fought
side-by-side to defend our nations and
the values we both uphold...'

HON. PHIL GOFF

To the People of the United States

New Zealand extends to the people of the United States our deepest sympathy for the loss of life from the terrorist attacks of September 11.

Most particularly, we share with the families and friends of victims their sense of loss and grief.

In the many conflicts of the twentieth century, New Zealanders and Americans fought side-by-side to defend our nations and the values we both uphold.

Confronted by this new threat, New Zealand commits itself fully to working with the United States and the United Nations to eliminate terrorism.

Terrorism poses a threat to the stability, security and prosperity of the whole world.

Only a united and determined response from the international community can defeat the evil that terrorism represents and ensure that peace, tolerance, human rights and the rule of law prevail.

Yours sincerely

Hon. Phil Goff
Minister of Foreign Affairs and Trade

PHIL GOFF IS MINISTER OF FOREIGN AFFAIRS AND TRADE AND THE MINISTER OF JUSTICE. HE IS MARRIED TO MARY AND THEY HAVE THREE CHILDREN. HIS INTERESTS INCLUDE FARMING, GARDENING AND SPORT. PHIL IS PATRON OF THE NEW ZEALAND YOUTH TRUST.

'..New Zealanders are foremost amongst
the friends of the United States...'

Message to the people of New York and America

New Zealanders are foremost amongst the friends of the United States.

While the physical distance between us may be great, the emotional ties are strong.

We all felt the pain as we watched so many suffer, but we also felt the pride as we watched how, in true New York style, people mustered up the courage to carry on with their daily lives.

We in New Zealand look to the strengths of America and applaud the message of President Bush that this free nation stands unbowed.

Yours sincerely

Hon. Bill English
Leader of the Opposition
MP Clutha/Southland

HON. BILL ENGLISH IS LEADER OF THE NATIONAL PARTY AND MINISTER OF PARLIAMENT FOR CLUTHA/SOUTHLAND. HE HOLDS A BACHELOR OF COMMERCE DEGREE, ENJOYS SPORT AND READING AND IS MARRIED TO MARY WHO IS A DOCTOR. THEY HAVE SIX CHILDREN.

'The warm friendship between New Zealanders and Americans goes back a very long way...This book of hope is a symbol of those enduring ties...'

To the American people

As a Kiwi who has spent many years working and living among you, I share your horror at the devastation of 11 September.

The hearts and minds and prayers of our family, as those of all New Zealanders, have been with you all, including especially the innocent victims and their loved ones, in the dark and challenging months which we have lived through since then.

If it is possible even to suggest that good can come out of those violent acts, it lies in the fact that the world has united under United States leadership as never before, to confront the tyranny of terror. As a result, the people of Afghanistan have been given renewed hope for a future free from violence, intolerance, persecution and hunger. New Zealand is committed to playing its full part in these endeavours.

The warm friendship between New Zealanders and Americans goes back a very long way. The events of September and the ensuing international developments have strengthened even further the bonds of friendship and cooperation between our two countries. This book of hope is a symbol of those enduring ties – and helping hands stretched out between friends in times of great need.

Warmest regards

John Wood
Ambassador

IN JANUARY 2002 JOHN WOOD TOOK UP THE POSITION OF NEW ZEALAND'S AMBASSADOR TO THE UNITED STATES OF AMERICA, BASED IN WASHINGTON DC. HE PREVIOUSLY SERVED AS OUR AMBASSADOR FROM 1994-1998. HE HAS HELD A WIDE RANGE OF POSITIONS IN THE MINISTRY OF FOREIGN AFFAIRS AND TRADE.

'Our common humanity... is our best hope for peace.'

Through life we all spend much time expressing in various ways how different we are from one another.

On 11 September 2001, differences disappeared. People of all races and creeds stood together as one great sorrowing family. We stood together for comfort.

What happened was too terrible to comprehend, yet in its aftermath each person we reached out to seemed more precious and deserving of our acknowledgement and respect.

Our common humanity – which has shone through with such brilliance in the days and weeks since then – is our best hope for peace.

God's blessings on the American people in this time of trial.

Rt. Hon. Jim Bolger
ONZ
New Zealand Ambassador
Washington

THE RIGHT HONOURABLE JAMES BOLGER, ONZ, SERVED AS PRIME MINISTER OF NEW ZEALAND FROM 1990-1997. MR BOLGER WORKED TO ENHANCE AND EXPAND US/NZ RELATIONS AS NEW ZEALAND'S AMBASSADOR TO THE UNITED STATES IN WASHINGTON UNTIL JANUARY 2002.

'I commend the courage and concern
for strangers, so selflessly, displayed
by Americans...'

New York is one of the world's great cities – it perhaps best represents the spirit of America.

I join the world in sending my sincere feelings of regret at the events that wreaked havoc in America on September 11th and my thoughts are with the people.

I commend the courage and concern for strangers, so selflessly displayed by Americans at the scene of the tragedies.

In this time of global unrest, the USA has embraced all those values that make it the great nation it is today.

May God bless America.

Hon. John Banks QSO
Mayor – Auckland City

HON. JOHN BANKS WAS ELECTED MAYOR OF AUCKLAND CITY IN 2001. HE HAS HAD AN EXTENSIVE CAREER AS A MINISTER OF PARLIAMENT. HE IS MARRIED TO AMANDA AND THEY HAVE THREE CHILDREN. HE WAS AWARDED THE QUEEN'S SERVICE ORDER FOR PUBLIC SERVICE IN 1990. (QSO)

MAYOR GARRY MOORE

I often use a proverb from our indigenous New Zealanders, the Maori, when I want to talk about what really matters in life.

The Maori say of life: 'He tangata, he tangata, he tangata' – 'It is people, it is people, it is people.'

Here in Christchurch on that day, the sudden urgent questions were all of people. Fathers, mothers, brothers, sisters, daughters and sons.

Our people. Your people.

Despite the distance of the physical journey our lives are all so close.

It's spring here. The miracle of the commonplace. A reminder that renewal is a reality.

Yours sincerely

Mayor Garry Moore
Christchurch

GARRY HAS BEEN THE MAYOR OF CHRISTCHURCH SINCE OCTOBER 1998. HE HAS A STRONG BELIEF IN STRENGTHENING COMMUNITIES AND EMPHASISING A MULTI-CULTURAL SOCIETY. GARRY AND HIS WIFE PAM SHARPE HAVE FOUR CHILDREN.

'Despite the distance of the physical
journey our lives are all so close...'

'..We here. You there. Brothers...
Every day you walk to Ground Zero
— we walk beside you...'

Back in '99 I landed in Newark. I was twenty-six hours' flight from my country of crashing waves, long grass, blue skies and magnificent mountains. Joe Rennish, a lieutenant in the fire department, ferried me to Flatbush Avenue – a fire-house in Brooklyn. There for over a month, I was continually welcomed by crew after crew. All heartening, hard, happy characters, brimming with good natured quips about themselves and their work.

Their generosity was shown without reservation. It demonstrated the strength of our brotherhood. Total faith in each other's unquestionable 'body on the line' for each other. Then, now and in the future it is so. We here. You there. Brothers.

So, you see, the fire-fighters down at Ground Zero – they are my friends. My family.

The fire-fighters – and New Yorkers in general – are a proud, strong, hospitable people.

They'll do what needs to be done and come up trumps.

We may be at the other end of the world from the fire-fighters in New York and America. But they are our people. And our brothers.

We know that this won't be over for the fire-fighters in New York until every last person's body is out of the smouldering wreckage. Until every last badge is found. It's respect for their fallen. They're still working. They'll still keep fighting. And while they are, we are.

Every day you walk to Ground Zero – we walk beside you.

We know you're already back on your feet and striding back to a more positive future than ever before. The patriotism of Americans will help make that come true.

And when the job is done, come to New Zealand to take a rest from it all. We have homes we can share with you. Our people have opened up their hearts and homes to you. You're family.

Warmest wishes

Murray
Fire-fighter

'Everyone is proud of the firefighters and New York; how brave they are.'

It was hard. It was sad for me to see guys who had been in the fire service for years and years – to see their hearts drop because their brothers had fallen. We did a parade. We had a service. We picked ourselves up again.

We sent messages.

It was good to see the public recognise that we represented the fire-fighters in New York too. In the first days people would toot and wave as they drove past our firehouse. They left flowers for our fallen brothers.

I am proud to be a fire-fighter. It is our job – our number one job – to help the public.

Everyone is proud of the fire-fighters and New York; how brave they are. They're not putting on a face. That's who they are. They're saying 'OK, this has happened. We can beat this. We can show the world. Yes, we have lost people, but this is our country and we are going to beat this'.

So that's what I think.

Best wishes

Sonny
Fire-fighter

MUZ, PUFF, SONNY AND AL

MUZ

You're our friends. Our brothers. If we could be there with you; taking one of your shifts off you we'd be there. From that first day you've never been alone – and you're not alone now.

PUFF

Keep on doing it brothers. We're with you.

SONNY

You have a winning attitude. We walk with you.

AL

Be strong. Hang in there. You're not alone.

MURRAY HAS GIVEN 29 YEARS OF SERVICE TO THE FIRE BRIGADE. HE HAS THREE CHILDREN AND FIVE GRANDCHILDREN. PUFF HAS BEEN IN THE SERVICE FOR 30 YEARS AND HAS TWO CHILDREN. AL HAS BEEN IN THE SERVICE FOR 31 YEARS AND IS MARRIED WITH TWO CHILDREN. SONNY IS NEW TO THE SERVICE AND IS EQUALLY PASSIONATE. HIS WORKMATES DESCRIBE HIM AS SONNY BY NAME, SUNNY BY NATURE. ALL FOUR FIRE-FIGHTERS ARE PASSIONATE ABOUT THEIR JOB.

'From that first day you've never been alone — and you're not alone now.'

'And when you're ready for a holiday there
are people here that will look after the
families of those firefighters, paramedics
and rescue workers — free of charge.'

ST JOHN AMBULANCE OFFICERS

Those of us who have been to New York remember the people and the place. It's so alive. The people are friendly too.

Because the ambulance paramedics in America are combined with the fire service there was not a lot of mention of their initial involvement at the scene of the tragedies. But we knew you were there.

Even though we're miles away we're affected by what you're going through. We're thinking of you. Talk to each other; be there for each other.

And when you're ready for a holiday there are people here that will look after the families of those firefighters, paramedics and rescue workers – free of charge.

We're right there with you.

Sincerely

Glenn, Sandy, Wayne and Annette
St John Ambulance Officers

THE ST JOHN'S AMBULANCE STAFF CONSIST OF 30% PAID WORKING STAFF AND 70% VOLUNTEERS. ON THE MORNING WE VISITED, THE TEAM PHOTOGRAPHED HAD JUST SAVED THE LIFE OF A PATIENT. THE SUCCESSFUL RESUSCITATION MADE THEIR DAY.

'...Don't be discouraged. We're thinking of you and we wish you well.'

Our thoughts go to Americans, especially the children who lost parents, those who lost loved ones and particularly the emergency care workers in New York.

Even though we've never experienced the horrific scale of tragedy that you had to contend with on September 11, we can relate to how you were thinking and what you were trying to achieve in saving lives – with little regard for your own. The magnitude of what you had to contend with is beyond words.

We'd like to say, don't be discouraged. We're thinking of you and we wish you well. You should be proud of the magnificent job you did and continue to do.

Best regards

Chris Wilding
Search and Rescue Helicopter Pilot

Mike Norman
Search and Rescue Ambulance Officer/Paramedic

CHRIS WILDING HAS BEEN FLYING FOR OVER 20 YEARS. HE FINDS THE MOST DEMANDING TASK IS HELICOPTER AIR AMBULANCE WORK AT NIGHT. CHRIS IS MARRIED TO SHARYN WITH THREE GREAT CHILDREN, WHOM HE SAYS, RULE THEIR LIVES.

MIKE NORMAN HAS BEEN AN AMBULANCE OFFICER FOR ELEVEN YEARS. HE HAS BEEN MARRIED TO HIS WIFE TANIA FOR TWELVE YEARS. MIKE SAYS THE HIGHLIGHT OF HIS LIFE – ASIDE FROM BEING MARRIED TO TANIA AND HAVING THREE WONDERFUL CHILDREN – WAS BEING ABLE TO GIVE A KIDNEY TO HIS SON OLIVER WHO IS NOW A THRIVING SEVEN-YEAR-OLD.

NEW ZEALAND
RED CROSS

'...People in action together create a
collective power that makes a very
real difference...'

The International Red Cross is a unique network that spans generations and links people around the world who all share a commitment to prevent and ease suffering, with a readiness to protect human life and dignity: no matter whose, no matter where, no matter when.

Members of the Red Cross were there on September 11 2001 and still continue their work beside firefighters in New York City, Washington and other areas of America today.

In acknowledgement of the tragedy that befell America and specifically its citizens, it is timely to reflect on the power of humanity. The reality is, that when we are united for a common cause, people in action together create a collective power that makes a very real difference to the lives of many people.

May we all, as an international community, continue to nurture the power of humanity by working locally and internationally to promote mutual understanding, friendship, co-operation and lasting peace among all people.

Our thoughts are with you.

Warmest regards

Kathy Ferigo
for New Zealand Red Cross
Canterbury West Coast Region

EMERGENCY RESPONSE VOLUNTEERS, KATHY COPLAND AND PATRICK VAN DER POL ARE TWO OF CANTERBURY WEST COAST REGION'S 118 EMERGENCY RESPONSE VOLUNTEERS WHO GAVE 16,200 HOURS OF SERVICE TO PEOPLE OF THE LOCAL COMMUNITY LAST YEAR.

LLOYD MATHESON

As a police officer in charge of a small South Island police station I have seen my share of tragedy.

Some years ago I was informed of a mid-air collision that involved two light aircraft flying over a fiord deep in the south. One aircraft plunged into the fiord and sunk to a depth of 300 meters. The second aircraft limped back to a local airport at Milford Sound. Because it was so remote, emergency service response to the incident was almost two hours away. It was a very traumatic time for all involved.

Reflecting on how we felt – it leaves me speechless to think how you must have all felt in response to the tragedies of September 11 in New York, Washington and Pennsylvania.

But what I can say is that the camaraderie and the close bonds that developed over our disaster down here in the south now over 11 years ago, is still significant to this day. Those bonds can never be broken. And you will find similar support and bonds in the years to come as it pertains to your situation.

The relationships forged at times like these between emergency services, government agencies, relatives, embassies, people in your country and people in countries all over the world, cement everlasting bonds of friendship and co-operation that have never been seen before and will bring the world closer. You're probably already experiencing this.

You have also shown the whole world how to lend support to your emergency services following this terrible event.

New York and the rest of America has shown New Zealand and the world how to rally against outrageous atrocities and stand united against attacks on your society – and this, we hope, will make for a better future for the world.

Kindest regards

Lloyd
Police Sergeant

LLOYD HAS BEEN A POLICEMAN FOR 34 YEARS AND IS ALSO A VOLUNTEER FOR THE LOCAL SEARCH AND RESCUE TEAM. HE MOST ENJOYS BEING ABLE TO HELP PEOPLE FROM ALL WALKS OF LIFE. LLOYD IS MARRIED WITH TWO CHILDREN. HIS SON IS A POLICEMAN IN INVERCARGILL AND HIS DAUGHTER LIVES IN LONDON. LLOYD LOVES THE NEW ZEALAND OUTDOORS.

'The relationships forged at times like these...cement everlasting bonds of friendship and co-operation that have never been seen before and will bring the world closer...'

VICTORIA FLIGHT

As a doctor I have looked into the eyes of many people suffering terrible loss and yet I have never felt as deeply moved by tragedy as I did when I thought of what you must be suffering.

September 11, the day that so many lives in America were shattered, is a day that will be remembered by people all over the world.

As a medical student I travelled through America – 22 States in a beaten-up VW van!

I will always hold dear my time in your country and my impression of Americans as a spirited and vibrant people.

You are truly very special.

Never forget your strength as people and as a nation.

Your spirit touches people all over the world.

Your spirit touches me.

Heartfelt wishes

Victoria

DR VICTORIA FLIGHT HAS BEEN IN GENERAL PRACTICE SINCE 1997. SHE HAS ALWAYS BEEN VERY INTERESTED IN NATURAL MEDICINE. SHE HAS A DAUGHTER WHO ENRICHES HER LIFE IMMEASURABLY.

'Your spirit touches people all over the world. Your spirit touches me...'

JOHN HAMILTON

This New Zealander

We are different you and I, yours and mine.

A good difference, a difference of friends intrigued by each other,
yet enjoying the bond of a common language, shared values
and a century or so of getting to know one another.

This New Zealander despaired at the TV images,
feeling powerless to help.
He wanted to stand and shout.

This New Zealander wanted to breathe the dust,
cut his hands and knees attacking the rubble
beside his friends in their need – rescuing together.

This New Zealander speaks for many.

We admire America, her vigour and confidence,
her resilience and generosity of spirit, and know it will not be spoilt.

Look to your friends – come to New Zealand – and be among them.

John
Secondary school teacher

JOHN HAMILTON SWAPPED A CAREER AS A BUILDER FOR THAT OF SECONDARY SCHOOL TEACHER SOME YEARS AGO. HE INSPIRES MANY OF HIS STUDENTS AND WHEN NOT TEACHING CAN USUALLY BE FOUND MANAGING AND CHAMPIONING THE SCHOOL ROWING TEAMS. HE AND HIS WIFE TRICIA HAVE TWO TEENAGE CHILDREN.

'Look to your friends — come to
New Zealand — and be among them.'

ROSLYN SCHOOL

Kia kaha (Be strong)

B e brave.
E verybody is thinking of you all.

S tart life again.
T ry your best to carry on.
R emember your loved ones lost.
O vercome your fears and troubles.
N ever give up.
G o forward and make a difference in the world.

We care.

On behalf of all of us here at Roslyn School
Palmerston North

ROSLYN IS A SMALL PRIMARY SCHOOL IN THE MIDDLE OF THE NORTH ISLAND. THIS SCHOOL HAS INSPIRATIONAL TEACHERS AND PUPILS WHO WORK ON CREATING A CARING ENVIRONMENT FOR ALL. THEY ALSO RUN A PROGRAMME CALLED "HIDDEN HEROES" INSPIRED BY THE BOOK ENTITLED 'KIWI TUCKER FOR THE SOUL'.

'We care.'

ROB AND SONIA WADDELL

To the people of New York and America.

As children growing up in New Zealand, we always dreamed of going to America. It was seen as the centre of activity and a symbol of greatness.

America portrays a patriotism that we as New Zealanders can identify with.

As athletes, we believe that this patriotism and spirit is what makes American athletes some of the most formidable opponents in the world.

Over the last couple of months we have seen how strongly united you are as a nation and it is truly inspirational. Be proud of your city and be proud of your country.

Whatever this series of tragedies has taken away from you, it will never take away your inner strength and courage.

Kia kaha, be strong.

Our compassion and our thoughts are with you.

Warmest regards

Rob and Sonia

ROB IS 3 X WORLD INDOOR ROWING CHAMPION, 2 X WORLD ROWING CHAMPION AND 2000 OLYMPIC GOLD MEDALIST IN THE SINGLE SCULLS. HE HAS A BACHELOR OF MANAGEMENT STUDIES DEGREE, IS A BLACK BELT IN JUDO, AND HE IS NOW SAILING FOR TEAM NZ IN THE NEXT AMERICA'S CUP.

SONIA TOOK UP A TRACK AND FIELD SCHOLARSHIP AT THE UNIVERSITY OF MINNESOTA, USA. SHE SWITCHED TO ROWING IN 1995 AND WAS A FINALIST AT THE SYDNEY OLYMPICS IN THE SINGLE SCULL AND A SILVER MEDALIST AT THE 2001 WORLD CHAMPIONSHIPS IN THE QUADRUPLE SCULLS.

'...we have seen how strongly united
you are as a nation and it is
truly inspirational.'

BERNICE MENE

I send my heartfelt thoughts to all families affected by the September 11 tragedy.

To me, America is a nation that is competitive in spirit and abundant with opportunities. You are world leaders in an amazing number of areas – a very go-ahead country.

As you carry on through these troubled times, I am sure that all of these sterling qualities will help keep you strong. Attitude is everything. Besides pride, loyalty, discipline, heart and soul, confidence is the key to all locks.

And as Americans you have the confidence and the spirit to carry on.

Warmest regards

Bernice

BERNICE IS A NATIONAL ROLE MODEL. SHE IS A MEMBER OF THE SILVER MEDAL WINNING COMMONWEALTH GAMES NETBALL TEAM, WAS THE FIRST CAPTAIN TO LEAD THE NEW ZEALAND NATIONAL NETBALL TEAM (SILVER FERNS) TO MULTIPLE WINS OVER AUSTRALIA, AND ALSO HOLDS A BA IN LINGUISTICS.

'...as Americans you have the
confidence and the spirit to carry on.'

'...be strong in the face of adversity, have hope for a better future and the confidence to go forward.'

SIR BOB CHARLES

As a New Zealander who spends extended periods of time in the United States, I wish to express my sympathy to the city of New York and all Americans who suffered the loss of family and friends during the recent terrorist attacks. The whole world has been affected by this great tragedy.

My message is to be strong in the face of adversity, have hope for a better future and the confidence to go forward.

As a golfer I travel extensively in the United States, including New York. I wish to assure you that these recent events will not diminish my desire to continue with the opportunities I have in the United States of America.

Yours sincerely

Sir Bob Charles

SIR BOB CHARLES HAS WON A GRAND TOTAL OF 75 INTERNATIONAL GOLFING TOURNAMENTS AROUND THE WORLD, INCLUDING THE OPEN CHAMPIONSHIP AT ROYAL LYTHAM ST ANNES. PROBABLY THE MOST SUCCESSFUL LEFT-HANDER TO PLAY PROFESSIONAL GOLF, SIR BOB HAS DESIGNED TWO 18-HOLE RESORT COURSES AND A NINE-HOLE COURSE IN NEW ZEALAND.

MARK INGLIS

I will always remember standing at the Statue of Liberty as a country lad from New Zealand, marvelling at the Manhattan skyline. I was fascinated by the thought of the thousands of people and personalities living their lives below it.

To the people of New York and America, although you'll never forget 'that day', please remember to use your strength of spirit to lift your heads and eyes, to look up and out to the future and to your way forward in strength together.

My thoughts are with you.

Mark

AFTER BEING CAUGHT IN A STORM FOR TWO WEEKS ON NEW ZEALAND'S HIGHEST MOUNTAIN 20 YEARS AGO, MARK INGLIS LOST BOTH LEGS TO FROSTBITE. SINCE THAT TIME HE HAS WON OLYMPIC SILVER IN BIKE RACING. MARK IS MARRIED WITH THREE CHILDREN AND WORKS AS A WINEMAKER IN MARLBOROUGH. HE RETURNED TO THE MOUNTAIN WITH GUIDE CHARLIE HOBBS IN DECEMBER 2001 AND AGAIN IN JANUARY 2002. MARK'S GOAL WAS ACHIEVED. ONCE AGAIN HE STOOD ON THE SUMMIT. HE IS A NATIONAL ICON.

'...Use your strength of spirit...
to look up and out to the future...
My thoughts are with you...'

MANDY JONES

No-one was unaffected by the tragedy of September 11.

It was as though our world stood still.

I had to keep reminding myself that it was not a movie.

And when I did the tears would not stop. I felt it from the heart.

It has brought us together – your country, our country and the world.

Through my experience as a nurse I can imagine there are some of you who have lost loved ones and may not be ready to hear messages of hope and inspiration for a while. I understand.

I think that unless you go through the event yourself you don't really know how it feels.

New Yorkers and Americans: I admire you for your patriotism, your passion and your openness. You allow people into your lives. It's very encompassing and welcoming.

Do keep open-hearted. Keep reaching out, keep communicating and helping one another.

Stay united.

And by doing that it will also help unite the world.

We send our love and prayers for a more peaceful world tomorrow.

Mandy
New Zealand Registered Nurse

MANDY HAS BEEN A REGISTERED NURSE FOR 19 YEARS AND CURRENTLY WORKS IN PAEDIATRICS AS SENIOR STAFF NURSE. SHE IS MARRIED WITH TWO CHILDREN AND COMMUTES FROM THE COUNTRY TO WORK IN THE CITY EACH DAY. SHE LOVES THE OUTDOORS AND SPENDING TIME WITH FRIENDS AND FAMILY.

'Stay united. And by doing that it will help unite the world.'

NOVA MONTESSORI SCHOOL

We don't want any people to hurt you or your families.

We want everyone in America and the world to be happy and kind to each other.

From the children
Nova Montessori School

NOVA MONTESSORI PRIMARY SCHOOL TEACHES A LOVE OF LEARNING AMONG ITS STUDENTS. THE SCHOOL WAS THE DREAM OF ONE OF ITS MAJOR FOUNDERS, PAULINE MATSIS. THE SCHOOL ROLE IS ALMOST ALWAYS FULL.

'We want everyone in America and the world to be happy and kind to each other.'

'...it is important for you to know
that there are people here... who care.'

STEPHEN TINDALL

I have regularly travelled to New York and over the years I have been impressed by the will to always improve and the huge progress that has been made in making New York a far safer place to visit.

As you now pick up the pieces from September 11 it is important for you to know that there are people here in New Zealand who care. We are with you in spirit at this very difficult time, as we are for all who have lost loved ones through terrorist activities.

My hope for the future is that all of us throughout the world will find a way to totally respect each other and work together to create a sustainable planet so everyone is able to enjoy a quality life on earth for thousands of years to come.

With warmest regards

Stephen

FOUNDER OF *THE WAREHOUSE* – ONE OF NEW ZEALAND'S GREAT BUSINESS SUCCESS STORIES. STEPHEN AND HIS WIFE MARGARET CREATED THE TINDALL FOUNDATION THAT DEMONSTRABLY ASSISTS MANY COMMUNITY PROJECTS IN NEW ZEALAND. STEPHEN ALSO FOUNDED AN ENVIRONMENTAL PROGRAMME CALLED ZERO-WASTE.

CHARLIE HOBBS

Dear friends in New York and America.

I've travelled to many amazing places on the planet on climbing expeditions and in the pursuit of adventure – including America. New York really was an adventure. I'd never been anywhere like that before – and I loved it.

It doesn't really matter where you go in the world. It's the life and spirit of the people that makes a place particularly special.

That's why Americans are so special to me. Your patriotism, the way you band together in times of adversity, the bravery displayed after that terrible day – there were so many outstanding acts of courage.

You showed the world that your spirit has not been broken – it's become stronger than ever. Now *that's* inspiring.

We flew the American flag from our office after September 11. It felt good to support our brothers and sisters in a far off nation. We stood proud knowing that you were holding your heads high – being strong.

You are family.

And it is true – we do walk with you – you're not alone.

Kia kaha (be strong).

Charlie
Adventurer & Mountain Guide

CHARLIE IS ONE OF NEW ZEALAND'S MOST HIGHLY RESPECTED MOUNTAIN GUIDES AND HAS COMPLETED MANY EXPEDITIONS IN REMOTE PARTS OF THE WORLD INCLUDING ANTARCTICA WHERE HE HAS MADE NUMEROUS FIRST ASCENTS. CHARLIE IS NOW BECOMING INVOLVED IN ADVENTURE FILMING. CHARLIE AND HIS WIFE MARY HAVE TWO GREATLY ADORED DAUGHTERS.

You showed the world that your spirit has not been broken — it's become stronger than ever. Now that's inspiring.'

BLAIR BROWN

Despair can be turned into strength.

New Yorkers and Americans, use the strength you have within to rebuild, regroup and recover.

You have friends walking with you.

Blair
Landscape designer

BLAIR BROWN HAS TRAVELLED THE WORLD AND LIVED IN MANY PLACES — INCLUDING NEW YORK. HE OWNS A LANDSCAPING DESIGN BUSINESS AND LIVES WITH WIFE KATE AND THEIR BEAUTIFUL NEW DAUGHTER. HE ENJOYS MEETING PEOPLE OF ALL ETHNIC ORIGINS AND BELIEFS, LOVES THE SOLITUDE OF THE NEW ZEALAND COUNTRYSIDE, FLY-FISHING AND SURFING.

'You have friends walking with you.'

ZED

There is so much about America that is special to us.

And over the past few months, as world attention has focused on New York, Washington, Pennsylvania and the rest of America, we have seen amazing images of love, courage and bravery.

Your true spirit has shone through.

We are thinking of you and pray that God will bless your nation, give you comfort and that despite the tragedy, people everywhere can reach out to create a more peaceful world for everyone.

With warmest wishes

Nathan, Ben, Adrian and Andy
Zed

ZED IS ONE OF THE MOST-LOVED ROCK BANDS IN AUSTRALASIA. THEIR FIRST ALBUM, SILENCER, WAS RELEASED IN 2000 AND ACHIEVED TRIPLE PLATINUM SALES AND PRODUCED SIX CONSECUTIVE HIT SINGLES. A NEW SINGLE HAS JUST BEEN RELEASED AND ANOTHER ALBUM IS IN THE PIPELINE.

'There is so much about America
that is special to us.'

'You... have moved beyond mere survival and have triumphed in the face of terrible adversity. I salute you.'

ANNAH

When I think of America one thing comes to mind. The document that shaped her history. A declaration of free will, indomitable spirit, independence and freedom.

Once more I see history repeating itself and see America in a time of strife.

Once more I see her ability and determination to re-assert herself.

Let this time too be a Declaration of Independence and Freedom.

Freedom from hate, from despair, from destruction and from terrorism.

Today I see that spirit at its best and I admire you for it.

Treasure your pride in your country above all else. Pride, love and determination will see America live on.

The true spirit of the country has risen with every life saved and with every effort made to save a life.

Like a phoenix from the ashes you shall rise and become stronger than before.

You – the Americans – have moved beyond mere survival and have triumphed in the face of terrible adversity.

I salute you.

Love Annah

ANNAH IS DEPUTY HEAD GIRL IN HER FINAL YEAR OF HIGH SCHOOL. SOME OF ANNAH'S ANCESTORS ORIGINALLY CAME AS IMMIGRANTS FROM EUROPE TO AMERICA. OTHERS WERE AMONG THE FIRST PIONEERS TO NEW ZEALAND. ANNAH IS PASSIONATE ABOUT SNOWBOARDING, SURFING, SPORT, FLYING AEROPLANES AND LIFE.

'The spirit and strength of character the
American people have shown... will prevail. It
is these qualities which will help you... always.'

STEVE BAYLEY

I commend the American people for shouldering such a hefty burden in these difficult times and send thoughts and prayers of compassion and strength with all my spirit and being.

With these words from across an ocean, I hope I can help provide you with a little added courage.

Some years ago I lost my leg in a car accident and not long afterwards I lost a great mother – so I understand something of personal pain and loss.

Those experiences took me into the unknown. I realised that there was a lot I didn't know. But I also realised that I could get through anything.

I started by doing what was possible for me. I got back into skiing. Since that time I have been privileged to represent my country in the winter paralympics.

For me, life became more precious. I see joys that I didn't see before. I try to go out and do more. To live life to the full. If you can do this, it can make a big difference, so I urge you to do this for yourself and your loved ones, including anyone dear to you that you may have lost.

The spirit and strength of character the American people have shown over the past few months, and which is in all of us, will prevail. It is these qualities which will help you, not just now but always.

I know that New Zealand and most of the rest of the world is with you, providing you with renewed encouragement to continue to live life to the fullest.

As we journey together through these troubled times I send my wishes for peace to all Americans and all people of goodwill on this planet. We all have it within us to live, love, forgive and make the world a better place for everyone.

Steve

AFTER LOSING A LEG IN A CAR ACCIDENT, STEVE BECAME A MEMBER OF THE NEW ZEALAND PARALYMPIC SKI TEAM. HE WON A GOLD MEDAL IN THE WORLD CUP DOWNHILL EVENT IN COLORADO AND THE DOWNHILL SILVER MEDAL IN THE 2000 DISABLED WORLD SKI CHAMPIONSHIPS IN ANZERE, SWITZERLAND. STEVE ALSO CONTRIBUTES TIME TO INSPIRING KIDS WITH TALKS IN SCHOOLS. HE LOVES THE OUTDOORS.

TODD BLACKADDER

My heart goes out to all the people in New York, the rest of America and the world who have lost loved ones in the recent terrorist attacks.

New Zealand stands alongside you.

We want to join nations around the globe, and people from all walks of life to try and build a more peaceful world.

Warmest regards

Todd
All Black Captain 2000

TODD IS ONE OF NEW ZEALAND'S MOST-LOVED RUGBY PLAYERS. HE REPRESENTED NEW ZEALAND AS AN ALL BLACK AND SERVED AS CAPTAIN IN 2000. HE IS CURRENTLY PLAYING RUGBY FOR SCOTLAND AND IS MARRIED TO PRISCILLA. THEY HAVE TWO CHILDREN.

'My heart goes out to all the people...'

'The only way to redress loss
is to somehow feel love again.
That we shall send you every day.'

LYDIA BRADEY

There cannot be anything so terrifying as someone seeking to hurt or destroy you. Many of us have closed our eyes and thought how awful it would be to lose our families in that way – the way of violence, anger and destruction.

It is so hard to overcome hurt and loss. The only way to redress it is to somehow feel love again.

That, we shall send you every day.

Love from the island in the Pacific.

Love for our planet.

Love is the best food in the world for human growth.

May you grow strong and tall on love.

Lydia

LYDIA IS A PHYSICAL THERAPIST AND MOUNTAIN GUIDE. SHE WAS THE FIRST WOMAN IN THE WORLD TO CLIMB MT EVEREST WITHOUT SUPPLEMENTARY OXYGEN. SHE DESCRIBES HER ASSOCIATION WITH THE MOUNTAINS AS PHYSICAL, INTELLECTUAL AND SPIRITUAL. SHE LOVED CLIMBING IN THE USA. 'THE PEOPLE ARE SO OPTIMISTIC, THE LANDSCAPE SO STUNNING, THE TORTILLAS SO FRESH!'

'The spirit of determination enjoyed by
the people of your great country will
win through...'

JOHN VON TUNZELMAN

To the Citizens of New York and America.

Although I have not visited New York I have, over the years, been interested to learn much about your very cosmopolitan and vibrant city, and was very shocked to think that man's inhumanity to man had been demonstrated again in such a cowardly fashion.

I have always regarded America as a land whose people believe in freedom and tolerance, as shown by the vast ethnic composition of its many people.

The spirit of determination enjoyed by the people of your great country will win through in future years as you join together to show the rest of the world that you will not be intimidated by fanatical cowards.

From the current series of events an even stronger nation shall arise to demonstrate to the world your commitment to freedom.

Best regards

John
National Park Ranger

JOHN VON TUNZELMAN HAS BEEN A DEPARTMENT OF CONSERVATION RANGER FOR 35 YEARS AND HAS ATTENDED MANY RESCUES AS A MEMBER OF THE VOLUNTEER SEARCH AND RESCUE CREW IN FIORDLAND. JOHN LOVES THE OUTDOORS AND HIS VOLUNTEER WORK FOR SEARCH AND RESCUE. HE IS MARRIED WITH TWO ADULT SONS.

'Together we'll move forward with you to help make the dream of a more peaceful world come true.'

BARRY MAISTER

I personally understand the horror that terrorism can inflict.

In 1972 there was terrorism at the Olympic Games in Munich. I remember clearly, and with much emotion, being part of the athletes' memorial gathering in the main stadium after the tragedy. To the utter delight of the 80,000 people gathered that day, it was declared 'the Games would go on'. We did not allow terrorism to win.

The Olympic spirit was protected with the decision to continue the Games and allowed it to burn brighter still. The Olympics embody hope, peace, sport for all, tolerance, freedom and excellence of endeavour. It is my belief that these are the very qualities that are encouraged and flourish in the very best of what America has to offer.

I was a visitor to New York some years ago and was impressed by its vitality, diversity and opportunity. I am sure that the spirit of the American people, the commitment you show to your country and what it stands for, will prevail as you look forward again.

The Olympic spirit denotes hope and promise. Even in the bleakest of times, the Olympic message is capable of uplifting, inspiring and strengthening the human spirit. The Olympic symbol consists of five interlocking rings which stand for the universal striving for a better and more peaceful world.

I look forward to visiting Salt Lake City early next year for the Olympic Winter Games, when that hope and promise will be manifest in the greatest sporting spectacle on earth.

Rather than dissuade us, the events in New York and the rest of America have refuelled our desire to achieve the goals of the Olympics.

I would like all Americans to know that your tragedy is our tragedy and the Olympic spirit is a universal and powerful force for healing.

Together we'll move forward with you to help make the dream of a more peaceful world come true.

Yours sincerely

Barry Maister
Secretary General of the NZ Olympic Committee

AFTER A DISTINGUISHED CAREER IN TEACHING, BARRY RECENTLY BECAME THE SECRETARY GENERAL OF THE OLYMPIC COMMITTEE. AN OLYMPIC GOLD MEDALIST HIMSELF, BARRY IS A MAN OF INTEGRITY WHO INSPIRES MANY. HE AND HIS WIFE CHERYL HAVE THREE GROWN CHILDREN.

JANE, SARAH AND FRASER SKINNER

We sat stunned as the events of September 11 unfolded. It was beyond belief and comprehension.

The most appropriate words we can offer are those spoken by your own President Abraham Lincoln on November 19, 1863, at Gettysburg:

'That this nation, under God, shall have a new birth of freedom, and that government of the people, by the people, for the people, shall not perish from the earth.'

With heartfelt best wishes

Jane, Sarah and Fraser

FRASER AND WIFE JANE PART-OWN THE COPPER CLUB, A FINE-DINING RESTAURANT IN QUEENSTOWN. AN EXPERT SKIER, FRASER IS ALSO CO-DIRECTOR OF AN INTERNATIONAL SKI RACE FOR CURE KIDS – A CHARITY HELPING TO FUND THE SEARCH FOR CURES FOR LIFE-THREATENING ILLNESSES FOR CHILDREN.

'...heartfelt best wishes'

'I fell in love with your vibrant, colourful
and energetic city, and its people.'

FATHER RICK

I spent nine months in New York in 1992 and 1993 and fell in love with your vibrant, colourful and energetic city, and its people. I made good friends and I can still see clearly in my mind many of the places of Manhattan.

I was always so impressed with the work of many of the churches in the inner city and have no trouble imagining your response to the suffering of your people.

I would like to extend to you, the people of New York and America, our love and our prayers.

The events on September 11 saddened us here at the Cathedral of the Blessed Sacrament Parish in Christchurch. The tragedy that unfolded before our eyes brought a deep response of love and prayers for the people of New York and America with a renewed commitment for us to pray for peace and justice in this troubled world.

God bless

Father Rick Loughnan
Cathedral of the Blessed Sacrament Christchurch

FATHER RICK LOUGHNAN GREW UP ON A FARM IN NEW ZEALAND. HE WAS ORDAINED AS A CATHOLIC PRIEST IN 1994 AND SPENT ONE YEAR OF HIS TRAINING AS A PRIEST AT ST JOSEPH'S SEMINARY IN NEW YORK.

THUBTEN JAMPA TULKU

A message of love and positive outlook

On the wings of long white clouds from New Zealand
– an island nation of peace in the blue Pacific –
that drift aloft heavenward to the people of New York and America
We send our love and prayers for a new beginning.

Just as the waters of our oceans merge into one taste
Let the people across the globe merge in haste
Into one human family, who whether here or there
march to the same direction,
A future of stability and peace.

As the moon of our virtues beams white light
May the blue lilies of great fortune bloom all bright
In the century 2000 and beyond, and in all countries,
Permeating the fragrance of a human understanding without any seam.

Thubten
Tibetan Buddhist Master

THUBTEN JAMPA TULKU IS A TIBETAN BUDDHIST MASTER. HE WAS BORN IN TIBET IN 1942 AND RECEIVED BUDDHIST TRAINING AFTER HE FLED TIBET, FOLLOWING THE DALAI LAMA'S FLIGHT INTO INDIA IN 1959. THUBTEN HAS ALSO TRAINED AS A TEACHER OF TIBETAN LANGUAGE AND CULTURE AND HAS TAUGHT TIBETAN CHILDREN IN INDIA FOR OVER 25 YEARS. HE CAME TO NZ IN 1996 TO TAKE UP THE POSITION OF THE BUDDHIST MEDITATION MASTER. HE LIVES IN DUNEDIN, NEW ZEALAND.

'A message of love and positive outlook'

'...Hand in hand we will make it through.'

On September 12 (New Zealand time) we woke to see the face of evil as clear as it may be seen.

We have witnessed 'graphically' a terrorist attack on the heart of western civilisation. It is right and proper that we should be deeply shocked.

As I watched the horror unfold on CNN, I could see and hear the numbing shock and disbelief people were experiencing. I could feel the same rising within me.

Such an event brings people to the very edge of coping. In our shock and in the face of such grief we are forced to the very boundaries of our understanding. It is the point where our assumptions about life come up against the hard edges of reality. The very faith that we all have 'deep down' in the essential goodness and wonder of life, seeks for acceptance, seeks for explanation and understanding and seeks for healing.

We need to touch the ground of our hope again.

And that hope is there! For we have been brought to the very heart of our faith by this evil. We may come to the realisation that we are not separate from this evil. President Kennedy expressed this reality for us when he said during the Berlin Blockade of the Cold War, 'Ich bin ein Berliner!' I am sure that many New Zealanders would want to join with me and say, 'I am an American! I am a New Yorker!'

Out of this experience we may also come to realise that humanity is not alone. That we are not isolated depending on our own strength to cope. We have a God who will bring us through this. Hand in hand we will make it through.

With warmest wishes

Reverend David Vaughan

FROM AN EARLY AGE DAVID KNEW HE HAD TO BE A MINISTER ALTHOUGH HE SAYS HE 'BUCKED THE CALL' FOR 25 YEARS. AFTER 14 YEARS AS A SECONDARY SCHOOL TEACHER HE BEGAN TRAINING AS A MINISTER IN THE PRESBYTERIAN CHURCH. HIS CHURCH CAN BE FOUND IN THE BEAUTIFUL WAKITIPU AREA OF THE SOUTH ISLAND.

'...There is, for each of us, enough joy, enough beauty, enough gaiety in the hours, if we will but treasure them.'

RABBIS DAVID AND PATTI KOPSTEIN

Hello to all our friends in America.

We are two Americans, living in New Zealand. In fact, we are the only Progressive Rabbis in all of New Zealand, serving the lovely congregation of Beth Shalom in Auckland. We live in the village of Devonport, overlooking Auckland harbour.

Our daughter in San Francisco phoned us in what was the middle of the New Zealand night to relay the awful news of September 11. Later that morning, a bouquet of flowers appeared on our back stoop. We are known as "the Americans" on our block and it was a simple but elegant expression of sympathy from one of our neighbours.

Our hearts go out to all of you for what you have suffered. We know full well what that suffering feels like as we have both lived in Israel and we have known many victims of terrorism.

The best thing to do is to now go on with our lives with even more vigour and resolve than ever before.

As the American Rabbi Joshua Liebman wrote, "Some children of earth are privileged to spend a long and sunlit day in the garden of the earth. For others that day is shorter, cloudier, and dusk descends more quickly as in a winter's tale. The day that we are privileged to spend...is not the same for all human beings, but there is, for each of us, enough joy, enough beauty, enough gaiety in the hours, if we will but treasure them."

We hope to see you soon. We are planning a visit in April. To us, that visit will be an act of patriotism and support for the people of New York and America.

In the meantime, may you learn to do what King David learned and recorded in the Book of Psalms, to turn your "mourning into dancing," to live even more deeply and meaningfully now, as you awaken and arise from your period of mourning. Treasure the hours!

With compassion, solidarity, and affection,

Rabbis David and Patti Kopstein
Devonport, Auckland

RABBIS DAVID AND PATTI CONSIDER THEIR GREATEST ACHIEVEMENTS TO BE THEIR SON AND DAUGHTER. THEY BOTH ENJOY THE OUTDOORS AND LOVE THEIR NEW HOME AND FRIENDS IN NEW ZEALAND.

'...we wish peace for the people in New York, America and all over the world.'

EMAD IBRAHIM AND FAMILY

We are a New Zealand Muslim family. The Muslim religion does not believe in murder. We join the world in its sorrow for the tragedies that occurred in America and we wish peace for the people in New York, America and all over the world.

Our very sincere wishes

Emad Ibrahim and family

EMAD IBRAHIM AND MONA SOLAMIN ARRIVED IN NZ SIX YEARS AGO FROM EGYPT. THEIR YOUNGEST CHILD WAS BORN IN NEW ZEALAND. EMAD PRACTISES AS AN ACCOUNTANT AND HAS DONE VOLUNTEER WORK FOR HIS RELIGION IN HIS NEW COUNTRY.

ANDREW MACDONALD

I've always enjoyed visiting America. You have led the world in many areas of technology through your commitment for the best.

The positive spirit of your country and your people has always made me feel that if anyone puts their best effort into achieving their dreams, they will indeed come true.

As a volunteer fire-fighter, coastal lifeboat rescuer and a volunteer minister for the Church of Scientology, I have always considered it a privilege to help others. I was half a world away when I heard news of the tragedies in America on September 11 – but I wanted so much to be there to help carry out any rescue needed – or to help those doing the rescuing in any way that I could.

The bravery of all the people at the scene was amazing – fire-fighters, paramedics, police, Red Cross, volunteer ministers – you all helped hundreds of people at Ground Zero and it was an inspiration to the rest of the world.

With the work that you all did providing such help to others you brought the world closer together and made it a triumph of the human spirit. Now – more than ever before – it is up to each one of us to continue that. We need to work towards making a better world for everyone regardless of colour, race or belief, by reaching out and being of the greatest help we can be to each other.

Warmest regards

Andrew
Engineer

ANDREW HAS TRAVELLED THE WORLD EXTENSIVELY. HE IS A MARINE ENGINEER AND HAS ALWAYS HAD A LOVE OF THE SEA. HE HAS BEEN A VOLUNTEER FIRE-FIGHTER AND HAS WORKED ON THE LIFEBOAT VOLUNTEER RESCUE SERVICE. FELLOW VOLUNTEERS HAVE FOUND HIS HELP INVALUABLE. HE HAS MANY AMERICAN FRIENDS.

*'With the work that you all did
providing such help to others you brought
the world closer... and made it a triumph
of the human spirit...'*

'Kia toa. Be brave.'

BRETT WALKER

Kia kaha. Be strong,

Kia toa. Be brave,

Kia manawanui. Be stout-hearted.

Arohanui.
Much love
Brett

BRETT IS A PERSONAL TRAINER, BODY BUILDER AND SUCCESSFUL BODY BUILDING COMPETITOR. BRETT'S PERSONAL GOALS INCLUDE HELPING YOUNG PEOPLE ENJOY DRUG-FREE, HAPPY LIVES THROUGH PHYSICAL FITNESS TRAINING PROGRAMMES. HE HAS TWO CHILDREN.

ALLISON ROE

In the face of adversity, Americans get on with it.

History shows that you are often the most generous, yet least appreciated people on earth.

America has provided opportunity and help to so many, has contributed billions in support and frequently forgiven billions more in debt.

I admire the resolve of the American people, that unconquerable spirit that dominates the thinking and attitude of a proud nation.

We can learn from you.

Continue to stand strong and triumphant.

We love you America.

Allison Roe
Winner of 1981 Boston and New York Marathon

ALLISON WAS AWARDED AN MBE – A MEMBER OF THE BRITISH EMPIRE FOR HER SERVICES TO SPORT. SHE IS A NATIONAL ICON. SHE WAS THE WINNER OF THE 1981 BOSTON AND NEW YORK MARATHON AND SET A WORLD RECORD AT 2 HRS, 25M 29s. SHE WAS THE NEW YORK COURSE RECORD HOLDER FOR 13 YEARS. SHE HAS TWO CHILDREN – DAUGHTER JORDYN (12) AND SON ELLIOT (9).

'We love you America...'

LLOYD WIGZELL

Over a long life I can say I have experienced my share of joy and sorrow.

It is hard for those of you who have lost loved ones. But through it all, if you can just keep boxing on and face the world with as much courage as you can muster up – a smile here and there – and a tune not far from your lips, it will help lead you to a brighter tomorrow.

Our thoughts are with you.

Yours sincerely

Lloyd

LLOYD LEFT SCHOOL AT THE AGE OF 13 TO HELP SUPPORT HIS WIDOWED MOTHER AND TWO SISTERS, MABEL AND EILEEN. HE WENT ON TO BECOME A VERY SUCCESSFUL AND WELL-RESPECTED BUSINESSMAN AND FARMER. HE HAS HAD A LIFE-LONG LOVE FOR HORSES AND TRAINED AND BRED CHAMPIONS. HE IS MARRIED TO PATRICIA AND THEY HAVE THREE GROWN CHILDREN.

'Our thoughts are with you.'

NIC KAGAN

The past has happened.

The future is unknown.

The present moment is all we have.

So let's put our honest best into it now.

Best wishes

Nic

SOME YEARS AGO DOCTOR NIC KAGAN HAD A LIFE-THREATENING BATTLE WITH CANCER. AFTER
TRADITIONAL METHODS OF DEALING WITH HIS ILLNESS FAILED, HE SOUGHT OUT HIS OWN CURE. PART OF
THE CURE FOR NIC INCLUDED DIET, MEDITATION, BUDDHIST CHANTING, AND WORKING AT WHAT HE
MOST LOVES TO DO: MOUNTAIN GUIDING, SKI GUIDING AND HORSE-TREKKING. NIC IS MARRIED TO JUDE.
THEY HAVE TWO DAUGHTERS.

'I love New York!'

MARGI ROBERTSON

I love New York! It has a spirit about it that no other city in the world can claim.

The buzz which comes from the people and the culture is unique, and for me it has become a necessity to visit whenever I make the journey to the Northern Hemisphere. And that hasn't changed – I'll still be visiting your beloved city whenever I can.

My heart goes out to all who lost loved ones as a result of the devastating events that occurred on September 11 – and the loss of lives of the innocent people who have been affected.

My hope for the future is that people of all cultures draw closer together and journey towards a new tomorrow in greater understanding and empathy.

Warmest regards from across the ocean.

Margi

MARGI IS A FASHION DESIGNER BASED IN DUNEDIN. HER LABEL – NOM D – CAPTURES THE IMAGINATION AND IS BECOMING VERY WELL KNOWN IN AUSTRALASIA, JAPAN AND EUROPE. MARGI COMES FROM A FAMILY OF EIGHT. HER PARENTS WERE REFUGEES FROM EUROPE – SHE HAS A UKRANIAN FATHER AND A GREEK MOTHER.

NADIA AND GED HAY

We saw the television images of the tragedy – feeling powerless to help from such a distance.

But even at the bleakest moments through it all the American flag flew high.

The strength of your spirit shone through as so many of you came to the aid of those in need, often risking your own lives to save others.

Be strong knowing that you are in the thoughts and prayers of people all over the world.

May you find strength and love in one another during this time of international challenge.

We send our warmest wishes of well-being to you and your families all the way from Queenstown, New Zealand.

Nadia and Ged

GED IS A VERY WELL-KNOWN ADVENTURER OF QUEENSTOWN. RECENTLY MARRIED, HE AND WIFE NADIA RUN MAD DOG RIVER BOARDING ON THE KAWARAU RIVER. THEY'RE BOTH PASSIONATE ABOUT THE OUTDOORS.

'We send our warmest wishes of well
being to you and your families...'

DAVE TAYLOR

Although I've never visited New York, thoughts of that amazing city always seem to conjure up black and white images of immigrant ships arriving in that huge harbour.

Ships at one time or another, crowded with refugees arriving from a war-torn or famine-stricken Europe to a country of hope and promise.

The immigrants brought with them stories of hunger and suppression. But they arrived in New York and America with dreams of creating a bright new tomorrow.

You've welcomed them, and together set about creating your country – America. That spirit on which your country was founded, that compassion your country has always demonstrated for others, can never be dimmed. Look to it.

It is with you now and will simply grow stronger, as you draw strength from each other – and from your friends throughout the world to re-build and walk together into a more peaceful tomorrow.

Our thoughts are with you.

Dave
Helicopter pilot

DAVE IS ONE OF THE MOST HIGHLY RESPECTED HELICOPTER PILOTS IN NEW ZEALAND. HE FLIES IN REMOTE MOUNTAINOUS AREAS OF THE SOUTH ISLAND AND HAS ALSO SPENT SOME YEARS AS A SEARCH AND RESCUE HELICOPTER PILOT.

'That spirit on which your country, was founded... can never be dimmed...'

'...our neighbours now come from around the globe.'

ERIN BAKER

September 11, 2001 marked a turning point in the world we know. No person will be left unaffected in some way, and now we must look to create a world where such acts of hatred will never happen again.

The world has become a small community, and our neighbours now come from around the globe.

We must look into our hearts, and as a collection of peoples occupying one planet learn to live and love more then ever before.

I cherish my life here as you all cherish your lives in America.

May peace unite us all throughout the world.

With warmest wishes

Erin

ERIN BAKER HAS BEEN WORLD TRIATHLON CHAMPION EIGHT TIMES AND HAWAIIAN IRONMAN CHAMPION TWICE. SHE WAS VOTED FEMALE TRIATHLETE OF THE DECADE IN 1990 BY A US TRIATHLETE MAGAZINE. ERIN LIVES IN CHRISTCHURCH WITH HER AMERICAN HUSBAND SCOTT MOLINA AND THEIR CHILDREN. ERIN IS A CITY COUNCILLOR AND A MEMBER OF THE DISTRICT HEALTH BOARD.

'Today I stand beside you.'

MICHAEL BURTSCHER

Yesterday I felt your pain

Then I saw your courage

Today I stand beside you.

Kind regards

Michael
Farmer

MICHAEL BURTSCHER FARMS 15,000 ACRES IN A REMOTE AREA OF THE SOUTH ISLAND. HE IS PASSIONATE ABOUT THE OUTDOORS AND ENJOYS SKIING, WINDSURFING AND HORSE TREKKING IN THE SURROUNDING MACKENZIE HIGH COUNTRY.

'It doesn't matter about your colour,
your race, or your religion — you have the
strength of spirit to rise to the occasion.'

I understand how anyone feels who has lost someone special and can feel for those whose lives have been shattered by losing loved ones.

I had a very dear friend I worked with called Betty Wark. We ran Narcanon together; a very successful programme that helps people get off drugs naturally, without using other drugs to do it. We worked hard and got some fantastic results. But just recently, Betty – who was 75 – became very ill. She said to me, 'Don't be sad about me. I'll be alright. Look after those who are living.' Betty passed on a few months ago. I was devastated.

There is strength in adversity though. Look for the good that comes out of tragedy too. You'll have met people you would never have otherwise met, shared with, or loved. There is an amazing outpouring of patriotism and call for peace that the world possibly hasn't known on this scale before. And strangers are reaching out to help one another.

It's a wakeup call for all of us on the planet really – put your hand out to others and care for them. It's about the bigger picture. It doesn't matter about your colour, your race, or your religion – you have the strength of spirit to rise to the occasion. We all do. And we will. We're with you – and all people in the world – on this journey for more peace – and we're with you in spirit through these tough times. Life is precious. Treasure it with those you're with and have the courage to move forward – because a brighter day will dawn.

Arohanui (big love)

Marina

MARINA HAS SEEN LIFE FROM THE BOTTOM UP. SOME YEARS AGO MARINA SUCCESSFULLY CONQUERED HER OWN DRUG ADDICTION THROUGH THE DRUG-FREE PROGRAMME NARCANON AND HAS WORKED HARD TO HELP OTHERS DO THE SAME. SHE IS NOW A PROUD GRANDMOTHER.

'From half a world away our
thoughts reach out to you all...'

VOLUNTEER CREW

We understand the dangers of rescue work.

From half a world away our thoughts reach out to you all –
especially our fellow rescue workers and their loved ones.

Yours sincerely

From all the volunteer crews
Sumner Lifeboat Institution

A GROUP OF LOCAL CITIZENS WHO WILLINGLY GIVE UP MUCH OF THEIR FREE TIME TO HELP OTHERS
IN DISTRESS.

MABEL AND BOB WELLS

We have never been to your country, but we feel for all who lost loved ones on that day of tragedy for New York, America and the world.

We know a little of loss. I was born in 1918 – the day my father was buried. My father died in the influenza epidemic after the First World War and my mother raised me and my brother and sister through the economic depression that followed. Our family had lost a dear father and husband.

Despite that, we made life special together.

We no longer had a father, but we did have each other. My sister Eileen and I had a wonderful mother and a great brother, Lloyd, who helped provide for us as the 'man' of our home.

My message to the people in America who have lost loved ones or whose lives have been shattered by recent tragedy, is to tell you I understand. I would like to encourage you to love the ones you still have and make life as special as you can. It is hard when you've lost those who are dear to you, but keep on loving; maybe it will just eat up some of the hatred in the world. Be strong. There is a brighter tomorrow.

We send our love.

Mabel and Bob Wells

NOW IN THEIR EIGHTIES, MABEL AND BOB ARE 'SALT OF THE EARTH' KIWIS. THERE ARE ALWAYS DELICIOUS AROMAS OF BAKING WAFTING FROM MABEL'S KITCHEN AND THE BAKING IS ALMOST ALWAYS FOR OTHERS. THEY HAVE THREE ADORED GROWN CHILDREN AND MANY GRANDCHILDREN.

'We encourage you to love the ones you still have and make life as special as you can... Be strong. There is a brighter tomorrow.'

ADAM

As I serve the coffees half a world away from New York and America, my thoughts and best wishes are with you.

I'm very grateful that the freedom of our democratic world continues to stand strong.

I wish peace and happiness for Americans and for all people on the planet.

Adam

ON MOST DAYS ADAM'S CHEERFUL FACE CAN BE FOUND AT ONE OF THE BUSIEST CAFES IN NEW ZEALAND. ADAM'S FUTURE GOALS INCLUDE MORE TRAVELLING AND SETTING UP HIS OWN CAFÉ ONE DAY.

'I'm very grateful that the freedom of our
democratic world continues to stand strong...
I wish peace and happiness...'

'From half a world away I want
to let you know we care.'

SEAN FITZPATRICK

The first time I travelled to New York I was completely overwhelmed. For me, it was like bringing the movies to life – things that I'd only ever seen on television: the high-rise buildings that make New Zealand's major cities seem like miniatures; the yellow cabs that you see in all the films; and the police officers riding around on Harley Davidson motorcycles – it all seemed so fascinating and so unbelievable.

When tragedy struck your amazing country I was deeply saddened. From half a world away I want to let you know we care. I send my best wishes for a more positive and peaceful future – for New Yorkers, Americans and everyone throughout the world.

With warmest regards

Sean Fitzpatrick
Captain of the New Zealand All Blacks
from 1992 to 1997

SEAN IS A GREATLY ADMIRED KIWI. HE REPRESENTED NEW ZEALAND AS AN ALL BLACK FOR 12 YEARS, AND AS CAPTAIN OF THE ALL BLACKS FROM 1992 TO 1997. HE PLAYED 92 TEST MATCHES – THE MOST ANY ALL BLACK HAS PLAYED. SEAN IS MARRIED TO BRONNIE AND HAS TWO DAUGHTERS.

RAY COLUMBUS

Hello New York. Hello America.

The USA has always been the symbol of freedom for me. At one time I lived in the San Francisco Bay Area for two years. I still return regularly.

My wife Linda and I honeymooned in America. The highlight was New York on Christmas Eve. We will never forget it.

We have so many true friends in America.

We now have family there too. Our daughter married a New Yorker. Our son-in-law and his father used to work in the World Trade Centre.

So you see – we are connected permanently. We're family.

For the first time in living memory the entire world has joined together. Hands and hearts across the water.

If we remain true to our basic values, if we love and respect each other, and teach our children these things, then God will bless us, and the world will be in good hands.

Our thoughts and prayers wing to you across the ocean.

We feel your pain, but we also feel your strength.

We are with you – every waking moment. Stay strong, we walk with you.

Remain positive.

For that is what makes you great.

Be.

Ray Columbus

23 November 2001

RAY COLUMBUS HAS WON EVERY MAJOR AWARD IN NZ SHOW BUSINESS AND WAS THE FIRST POP STAR IN THE BRITISH COMMONWEALTH TO BE AWARDED AN ORDER OF THE BRITISH EMPIRE. HE HAS HAD OVER 14 HIT RECORDS AND TOURED IN CONCERT WITH ROY ORBISON, THE ROLLING STONES AND MANY OTHERS. RAY IS MARRIED TO LINDA. THEY HAVE THREE CHILDREN DANIELLE, SEAN AND TINA. TINA LIVES IN BOSTON.

'Stay strong, we walk with you.
Remain positive. For that is what
makes you great...'

'I believe that the spirit of America can rise above tremendously difficult times and go on to prosper and grow...'

NADENE

I believe that the spirit of America can rise above tremendously difficult times and go on to prosper and grow – spiritually, emotionally and financially.

History has proven this too.

My message to help you at this time is to encourage you to devote your attention to what is positive and within your control. Be true to your heart. Keep moving steadily forward, even when circumstances seem to be working against you – for that is when you can make the most meaningful and positive differences in all areas of life.

My wishes for a more peaceful world for you all in America and for everyone.

Warmest regards

Nadene

NADENE OWNS AN ART GALLERY IN THE QUEENSTOWN AREA. SHE LIVES WITH HER PARTNER AND SON AND IS PASSIONATE ABOUT ART, THE OUTDOORS AND PEOPLE.

'We reach out from half a world away
and join with you in your resolve to
create a more peaceful future for all.'

PETER KENT

The events of September 11, 2001 will remain forever etched in the collective memory of humanity.

The World Trade Centre's twin towers each had a square plan of 63 metres by 63 metres and were 110 stories high. They made a magnificent sight shimmering in the morning light. Within 105 minutes both towers were gone.

The scale of the tragedy was unimaginable.

We reach out from half a world away and join with you in your resolve to create a more peaceful future for all.

Our thoughts are with you.

Peter
Architect

PETER KENT HAS BEEN AN ARCHITECT FOR 25 YEARS, IS A MEMBER OF THE NEW ZEALAND INSTITUTE OF ARCHITECTS AND HAS WON LOCAL AND NATIONAL AWARDS FOR ARCHITECTURE. HE IS MARRIED TO JANE PARKER AND THEY HAVE TWO CHILDREN.

'I am half a world away, thinking about New York.'

I am half a world away thinking about New York.

I know your spirit is indomitable.

I see New York as the global capital that champions the cosmopolitan mix as a microcosm of our planet.

The city that celebrates the texture of multi-cultural diversity, fantastic architectural icons: the Statue of Liberty that espouses freedom; the Guggenheim Museum that celebrates culture and history; the Brooklyn Bridge that shows strength.

But what I admire and respect most of all in the average New Yorker is your eclectic mix of wonderful fashion and culture that celebrates the individual – but with the assurance of anonymity.

So here I am – on the other side of our globe – thinking about New York.

And I know that the future will be good.

New Yorkers will always be the colossi that arise from the ashes of adversity.

The people of your city couldn't – wouldn't – do it any other way.

Heartfelt regards

Mike
Hairdresser

MIKE HAMEL HAS WON NEW ZEALAND MASTER HAIRDRESSER OF THE YEAR FOR THE PAST TWO CONSECUTIVE YEARS. HE IS MARRIED TO GLENYS AND HAS TWO CHILDREN WHOM HE SIMPLY ADORES.

'We were uplifted by the spirit of New Yorkers and Americans. You are an inspiration to the rest of the world.'

CRAIG NORGATE

New Zealanders were shocked and horrified by the tragic news of the terrorist attacks in the United States on September 11 – but we were also uplifted by the spirit of New Yorkers and Americans.

America was wounded by these attacks but has recovered and is emerging stronger and more united than ever.

You are an inspiration to the rest of the world.

Craig Norgate
Chief Executive Officer
Fonterra Co-operative Group Ltd

CRAIG NORGATE IS THE CHIEF EXECUTIVE OFFICER OF FONTERRA — NEW ZEALAND'S LARGEST DAIRY EXPORTER. HE IS ALSO A DIRECTOR OF THE NZ RUGBY FOOTBALL UNION. CRAIG HOLDS A BACHELOR OF BUSINESS STUDIES IN ACCOUNTING AND FINANCE AND LIVES WITH HIS FAMILY IN AUCKLAND.

ANSJA AND MARK

ANSJA

It is my hope that all of us in the world reach out to help you carry your tragic loss of September 11 and we work together to create more and more happiness on our planet.

With love

Ansja

MARK

The devastation on September 11 has challenged our emotions.

We must now deal with this enormous loss and continue forward to achieve as much as we can in life and to appreciate the joy and privilege of waking up and starting each new day.

Warmest wishes

Mark

ANSJA HAS ACCOMPANIED MARK ON SEVERAL HIMALAYAN EXPEDITIONS AND IN THE FUTURE IS LOOKING FORWARD TO TAKING THEIR TWO SONS THERE TO MEET THE PEOPLE.
MARK IS A VETERAN OF MANY HIMALAYAN EXPEDITIONS AND HAS SUMMITED THE NORTH SIDE OF MOUNT EVEREST TWICE. HE LIVES WITH PARTNER ANSJA AND THEIR TWO SONS, TAANE AND NIKAU AND HAS RECENTLY BECOME VERY INVOLVED WITH ADVENTURE FILMING.

'We must continue forward to achieve as much
as we can in life and to appreciate the joy
and privilege of starting each new day.'

ANDY BRINSLEY

Half a world away, you are not so far.

That Day the dust and ash fell on us all.
We became fellow villagers.

For those who lost their lives *That Day*,
For the black hole in your city
– we shall never forget.
But don't keep looking in.
There are no answers.

Harness *That* emotion.
Intensify *That* spirit.
Recharge *That* special energy
we know as New York and America!

Warmest regards

Andy

ANDY IS A FOUNDING MEMBER OF THE WORLD FAMOUS AJ HACKETT BUNGY CREW. IN 1994 HE STARTED
PIPELINE BUNGY AND IS CURRENTLY A DIRECTOR OF KAWARAU JET – THE WORLD'S FIRST COMMERCIAL
JETBOAT OPERATION. ANDY AND HIS WIFE CLAIRE HAVE TWO CHILDREN, POPPY AND WINSTON.

'Intensify that spirit. Recharge that
special energy, we know as New York
and America!'

'...we have faith that those qualities that make Americans great will help you to emerge with hope and courage for the future.'

ARCH AND JANE CAMPBELL

To the people of America.

Our hearts and our thoughts, as a family, have been with you in the past months as we imagine the sadness that has so shockingly disrupted your lives.

As individuals, and as a nation, we in New Zealand have been influenced and benefited in countless positive ways by the ideals and energy that make your nation and your people great and unique. We have come to share many philosophical and cultural perspectives that make us feel particularly close in times of joy and of distress.

We have seen so much to admire in the way that you have worked together in this crisis and we have faith that those qualities that make Americans great will help you to emerge with hope and courage for the future.

We have found courage in dark times from the following thoughts which we send to you.

Keep your faith in beautiful things
In the sun when it is hidden
In the spring that follows winter
In the harvest from the winter earth
In the strength of the human spirit.

We send our love to you all.

Arch and Jane

ARCH AND JANE OWN A VERY SUCCESSFUL FOOD FACTORY. THEY HAVE THREE CHILDREN. DAUGHTER SARAH IS A NATIONAL MARKETING MANAGER OF NZ FOODS. SON BEN IS A MEMBER OF THE NEW ZEALAND ROCK GROUP ZED AND THEIR OTHER DAUGHTER BETH IS A MEMBER OF THE BACKCHAT BARBERSHOP QUARTET THAT RECENTLY WON A WORLD CHAMPIONSHIP.

VICKY MCLENNAN

Congratulations New Yorkers!

You are teaching young people all over the world the importance of courage, determination and perseverance in times of adversity. The comfort and support you have offered each other and the faith and confidence with which you embrace the future will be an inspiration to generations to come. America's indomitable spirit lives on.

The students I work with were stunned, appalled and then touched by your tragedy. I see in them a new awareness and compassion and a firm resolve to forge a more harmonious destiny for mankind.

We share your anguish and rejoice in your unyielding hope and optimism.

Vicky
Head of Senior College
Christchurch

VICKY MCLENNAN HAS BEEN INVOLVED IN THE EDUCATION OF YOUNG PEOPLE FOR 20 YEARS. SHE IS CURRENTLY THE HEAD OF A SENIOR COLLEGE IN CHRISTCHURCH. SHE HAS ALSO BEEN A DANCE TEACHER, CHOREOGRAPHER, AEROBICS INSTRUCTOR AND A KEEN RUNNER. SHE HAS TWO TEENAGE CHILDREN.

'America's indomitable spirit lives on.'

Kia kaha – be strong

DAN AND BRYAN

Kia kaha.

Be Strong.

Dan and Bryan
Drainage Crew – Calcon Asphalt

DAN AND BRYAN. A COUPLE OF VERY OBLIGING DOWN-TO-EARTH KIWIS WHO CAN BE FOUND AT VARIOUS CONSTRUCTION SITES AROUND CHRISTCHURCH.

143

REBECCA

I send my love to all the children in America and the world.

I like to think of the world as one big family.

It doesn't matter what differences we may have in religion, colour or beliefs – just as long as we don't hurt each other.

So – I look towards tomorrow and wish for peace and happiness in America – and the world – on a planet that has learned to make room for kindness. And love for one another.

Will everyone help me make that tomorrow today?

With love from

Rebecca

REBECCA BEGINS HER FIRST YEAR AT HIGH SCHOOL IN 2002. SHE LOVES ANIMALS AND ENJOYS PLAYING THE VIOLIN AND NETBALL. SHE IS ALSO VERY INTERESTED IN ART, CULTURE, AND ARCHITECTURE.

'I look towards tomorrow and wish for
peace and happiness... Will everyone help
me make that tomorrow today?'

Thank you

The following pages acknowledge the very special people who made this book possible.

ACKNOWLEDGEMENTS

The birth of any book we publish involves a team of people working with us who share the dream to create something very special. But this particular book was not part of any planned project. It started with a strong desire to help. It began with an idea and no budget. As we are a very modest company of four, we needed some assistance. We asked many people to contribute in terms of time and skills — at least until we sold some copies of the book. Even though there was no budget and no time, several people stepped forward. They came forward because they also cared about the people in America. They wanted to help. And they did. The people on these pages are our knights in shining armour with very big hearts.

OCEAN DESIGN

I approached several of New Zealand's top design companies, gave them a brief and asked if they were able to work with us and contribute the cost of the design work — and deliver before Christmas. It was an impossible request really. All of the design companies we asked loved the concept but were busy - including Gary Stewart and his team at Ocean Design. But the Ocean Design team was as passionate about this book as we were. They worked with us at crazy hours of the day and night to make our vision for the book a reality, they understood our need to do justice to the messages and photos and they treated us like their most important clients. Their professionalism, care and big hearts have taken our breath away. They didn't miss a beat. Gary and Ocean Design: we salute you. Thank you so much for helping to make this book come true.

TRADESCANS

Andrew Budd runs a family company producing scans of the highest quality. He is always in great demand. When we told Andrew about the project, he wanted to help, and worked late into the night to make it happen. Without his scans the task would have been very difficult. Andrew — thank you so much for such a stellar job and your generous help.

RANGIORA PRINT

The printing of any book is the largest expense. Although we have good contacts in the printing industry, it is a daunting task to find a company willing to print a high quality book on no budget. Rangiora Print came through with a quote at cost which was fantastic at such short notice. Rangiora Print is a family business, built up by Jim Clayden and his wife Helen. Jim has had a battle with his health recently but he is still in there pitching, and he wanted very much to contribute to this project. Helen, Brett and the team at Rangiora Print — a sincere thank you.

LYNDA ACKLAND AND VICTORIA WIGZELL
— AT THE COALFACE OF NEW ZEALAND OUTSIDE

It isn't unusual for our team at the office to arrive at work and be faced with a new project that — although guaranteed to be inspiring and exciting — becomes quite daunting when added to an already busy work-load. Our intrepid office team, Lynda and Victoria, have been of incredible help in making this book happen. As my personal assistant, Lynda has relayed and chased up countless loose ends and details that were vitally important. Victoria, our new office assistant, has spent extra hours proof-reading, driving and relaying messages. They have given of their best as a way of sending their warmest wishes to their unknown friends in America. You're a formidable team to have in the office. Heartfelt thanks to you both.

ROB GREENAWAY

Every editor needs an assistant editor, and Rob is my mainstay in this department. During the course of this project he has turned up at all the right times to set me straight, offer his sage advice and steer me back on course if necessary. When I approached Rob he was up to his ears in consultancy work, but he contributed precious hours he could scarcely spare — because he believed in the project and wanted to help. He too wishes a more peaceful world for all.

PHOTOGRAPHERS

The following photos were shot by Mary and Charlie. Each person was asked if they would look straight into the lens, think of their unknown friends in America and send their warmest wishes. They did.

MURRAY JAMIESON, SONNY, FIREFIGHTERS, ST JOHN AMBULANCE OFFICERS, THE PARAMEDICS; CHRIS AND MIKE, THE RED CROSS, DOCTOR VICTORIA FLIGHT, JOHN HAMILTON, ROSLYN SCHOOL CHILDREN, MANDY JONES, NOVA MONTESSORI SCHOOL, CHARLIE HOBBS, MARY HOBBS, BLAIR BROWN, ZED, ANNAH, FRASER SKINNER AND FAMILY, FATHER RICK, THUBTEN JAMPA TULKU, REV.DAVID VAUGHAN, EMAD IBRAHIM AND FAMILY, ANDREW MACDONALD, BRETT WALKER, LLOYD WIGZELL, NADIA AND GED HAY, DAVE TAYLOR, ERIN BAKER, MICHAEL BURTSCHER, SUMNER LIFEBOAT INSTITUTION, MABEL AND BOB WELLS, ADAM, PETER KENT, MIKE HAMEL, MARK WHETU, ANSJA AND NIKAU, ANDY BRINSLEY, ARCH AND JANE CAMPBELL, VICKY MCLENNAN, DAN AND BRYAN, REBECCA.

PHOTO SPORT: ROB AND SONIA WADDELL, SEAN FITZPATRICK AND ALLISON ROE
NEIL LEVERSEDGE: MARINA SELLERS
EUGENIE OMBLER: NIC KAGAN

A special thank you to Photosport for permission to print the photo of Rob and Sonia Waddell free of charge in this book and a special thank you to Eugenie Ombler for permission to print the photo of Nic Kagan as a contribution towards this book.

OTHER PHOTOS THAT APPEAR HERE HAVE BEEN KINDLY LENT FROM THE PRIVATE COLLECTIONS OF THE INDIVIDUALS PHOTOGRAPHED.

TO THE PEOPLE WHO APPEAR IN THIS BOOK

One of the greatest privileges in making this book was meeting the people that appear in it. Each person was more than willing to give up their time. Each person genuinely cared, and each person wanted to communicate their messages from half a world away. We were humbled by the passion and the spirit of these amazing New Zealanders and have been honoured to be able to bring you their messages.

To the people in this book – a very sincere thank you for taking the time and being willing to share your care and compassion with the American people.

'Never forget your
strength as people and
as a nation.
Your spirit touches
people all over the world.
Your spirit touches me...'

'Look to your friends
— come to New Zealand
and be among them'

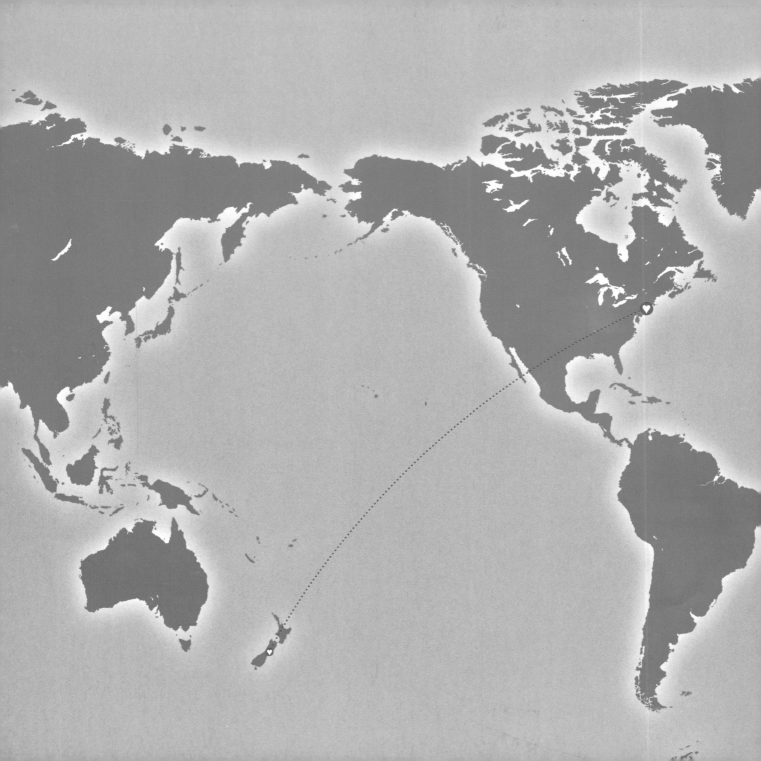